"Alex Forbes, Canada's finest poet, brings us yet more sweet delight." -- *Bette Shippam, University of British Columbia*

"*After the moon a blue ocean* shimmers with quiet brilliance. The poet's voice - both rooted in and freed by form - sings into being a mosaic of magical images all woven together by the flight of bees. This quiet revolving of ideas is constant yet always a surprise, something like the moon's own path." —*Deanna Barnhardt Kawatski, best-selling author of* Wilderness Mother, Clara and Me, Stalking the Wild Heart, *and upcoming* Burning Man, Slaying Dragon.

"To paraphrase one of Forbes' own poems, these are

> tiny poems
> pregnant with
> giant children"

—Rebecca Jacobson, Professor of English, Selkirk College.

"Forbes captures the winsomeness of an image . . . creating poems that sometimes startle and always delight."—*Kay McCracken, Co-founder, Shuswap Lake International Writers' Festival; author,* A Raven in My Heart.

after the moon a blue ocean

contemporary haiku and
other poems

alexander forbes

Red Heifer Press

AFTER THE MOON A BLUE OCEAN: Contemporary Haiku
   and Other Poems.
Copyright © 2012 by Alexander Malcolm Forbes.
Published in the United States of America by Red Heifer Press,
P.O. Box 1891, Beverly Hills, California 90213-1891.
All rights reserved.

Cover art by Natalia Vanessa
Graphic layout and design by Red Heifer Press

Library of Congress Control Number: 2011944213

ISBN: 978-0-9631478-7-5

Table of Contents

Acknowledgments

Some of the poems in this volume and the companion volume, *luminous orange*, forthcoming from Red Heifer Press, have appeared in the following: *Modern Haiku* (Madison, Wisconsin); *Frogpond* (New York); *Fan* (Atlanta); *Woodnotes* (Foster City, California); *RAW NerVZ* (Aylmer, Quebec); two catalogues of joint gallery exhibitions with Tricia Sellmer: *Double Exposure* (Burnaby, BC: Cap-à-Pie, 2004), and *boppin' with Mr. Mynah* (Fort Nelson, BC: Phoenix Theatre, 2007); and on a CD album entitled, *the beauty of the city in the last hour of the night*, a cycle of poems by Alexander Forbes, set to music by Henry Small, Capitol Records Gold Record recipient, former lead singer of PRISM, and the producer of the album; and read by actor/singer Tina Moore, one of Canada's most accomplished performing artists, known to many viewers for her acting in the Leo and Gemini Award-winning series, *The Vetala*. For her cover painting inspired by the title poem of this collection, my admiration and my thanks to Natalia Vanessa, truly a rising star in the Canadian art world. Her delightful illustrations and cover art for my novella, *Oranges* (Gracesprings Collective, 2010) were showcased with the book throughout the 2010 Olympics at The Oracle, in Whistler.

for Susan

Foreword

This volume, like its companion volume, luminous orange, is comprised of poems written in four of the forms English poetry has inherited from Japan: haiku, senryu, tanka, and haibun.

For a long time, the English language haiku was written with syllable counts of five, seven, and five respectively in its three lines. This practice was based on the structural divisions in traditional Japanese haiku, as marked by onji – the fundamental metrical unit in Japanese. And the same may be said of senryu – the whimsical cousin of haiku that is formally, if not thematically, the same as haiku.

In recent years, however, a number of traditionalists have questioned the wisdom of maintaining too strict a correspondence between onji and the English syllable. Not only are the two not simple equivalents, but it has been found that a haiku of seventeen syllables in English takes on average longer to read aloud than a traditional Japanese haiku. Due to the differences between Japanese and English, numerical parity does not achieve equivalence in duration, and a slightly different effect results when duration is altered. With this in mind, some traditionalists now suggest that haiku and senryu written in English should in fact be written using fewer than seventeen syllables, with shorter lines.

In the present volume, and its companion volume, examples of both kinds will be found as well as poems that owe their ultimate origins not only to free verse and other more recent experimental developments in English poetic practice, but also to the New Trend Haiku Movement that began a century ago in Japan, a movement away from the requirement of seventeen sounds and also from other traditional requirements such as a seasonal word or image – a current of free verse, as it were, in the sea of Japanese forms.

Tanka – a five-line poem that follows a haiku/senryu pattern in the first three lines before concluding with two additional lines (each traditionally the length of the second line) – is also represented here. So too is haibun, prose historically accompanied by haiku. Needless to say, the observations above also apply to these forms, and both to my traditional and to my experimental work with them in this and the companion volume.

A final note: the haiku beginning "fallen bowgh" is written in Middle English, a language used here for the musical possibilities it provides.

Alexander Forbes

1 after the moon a blue ocean

hollow smile –
Russian doll pregnant with
wooden children

fallen bowgh
couvred by rayn in
Aprill floures

every morning
after the moon –
a blue ocean

empty classroom –
where it's always
the end of June

what bee

ever caught up

to itself

bee hive –
where summer repeats
its own stories

moonlight
turning rosebushes
into shadows

forgotten letter
folded in my pocket –
space bent by time

morning frost –
grass ready for the weight of
red apples

goldleaf continents
set in a blue globe –
summer beaten thin

painted china

1

tea cup painted in
China   when China still
had emperors

2

painted scene holding tea
better than China retained
its emperors

3

touching a snow-covered
palace - only to feel
warmth

2 two tanka

first of the month −
when all across town
men struggle with
boxes of long overlooked
National Geographics

when snow turns to rain
and mists are the only petals
on the dark rosebush
the hasty observer,
seeing gray, senses – red

3   three haibun

The rain water that filled the garden urn did not freeze completely last night, before the snow began to cover everything. Snow on ice, ice on water: the green container that once held summer, now a white container of winter.

when the blackbird flies
into the cold sky between
the gray clouds

At dawn, the used car lots become almost poetic in the rain: but the poetry has nothing to do with the car lots *as car lots*.

Rain is poetic in itself, as dawn is, whereas the car lots are of course inherently unpoetic. Nor does their location in a run-down suburb of Vancouver do anything to alter the fact. The poetry could be explained simply as the rain, or as the dawn. But rain at dawn is even more suggestive, for another kind of poetry is evoked here: one that depends upon relationship. That's how the car lots get in, despite themselves.

From this we are able to recover theories of aesthetics that were of importance to the Romantics: theories of the ordinary, and of association. The ordinary recalled quietly, and then seen in perspective.

It will be association and perspective that unexpectedly stops more than a few of the residents of the neighboring apartment buildings, during the day when they are away at work. They will share something with each other, without knowing it: in pauses, when they recollect what they had seen. First thing in the morning. From their windows.

rainy street at first
light – car lots and one thousand
apartments

It's already the 18th of August but I want to be in Vancouver before the end of the month, to revisit a day fifty years ago that now is entrusted to me. Why else did two strangers to each other give me, years apart, two halves of a single story: the locations that allowed me to draw the only line Elvis could have walked from the tracks behind the railway station on Main, to Portland Al's grocery store? A line defined by an intersection, and dead end streets.

Who, besides me, would be there in the morning to reconstruct the time Elvis spent alone in Vancouver, his forgotten walk on August 31st, 1957?

You know what? I suspect I will *see* Al again, though if I do it might be for the last time in this world. He is very old now. But that day meant enough to him that he probably will return to the corner where his store used to be, one way or another.

But if not this year, then next perhaps – for the last day of August will always be an anniversary for Al, though only this one will be the fiftieth. And I will return if need be – next year if I have to.

Wouldn't that be a found poem? Walking up from the rail yards, remembering Elvis, but finding Al?

There's more than one metaphor possible here, and a whole lot of diesel smoke and memory. A lot of shaking still going on.

> at the red light –
> a convertible
> playing Elvis

4   outside the window

green shoots –
a garden growing
underground

birds do not know
their Latin names but
sing anyway

it's a promising
morning when children run for
the school bus

arithmetic class –

where numbers play games but also

keep their promises

sharp eyed teacher
beats time with chalk   marches pupils
across short poems

children's poetry

class   counting syllables to

the stamp of short feet

back lanes at first light –
where the sun will soon discover
its corridors

(green) the playground
beneath (first) light

– and the red swings!

cat using her
entire body to ask
a single question

walking toward

the blue mountains

the green mountains

at a highway pullout –
waiting for the sun to be
born in the mountains

dawn and the river
carrying gold down
gray waters

souvenir store –
where a forgotten town sells
memories of itself

long line of beaches –

and the white glare of
morning

through the train
window her small
dusty relatives

paper skins –
where onions write their
own stories

bee in

the kitchen   a small price

to pay for summer

bees — ruptures of
syntax   in sentence,
and westward

sunny bees
flying radiantly through
the ultraviolets

what were the poems of

Babe Ruth but long lines carried

home on short feet

looking out the bus
window at the street you crossed
one hour ago

leaping

fish,   commas in the long

sentence of the river

stories all around us

twelve birds chattering
on the phone line just above
the broken fence

it's all language
though you have to be
in on the stories

too many
stars to fit my
horoscope

frescoes of

the moon   wide as

the ocean

small town
on the prairie   waiting for
the moon

desks propelled
by sixty feet –
school resumes

rejoicing with
the children at
the puppet show

silent

ventriloquist   fidgety

puppet

book bus
driving Mozart's letters
all over town

.

shadows of leaves
falling across the bend of
the river

somewhere in

the orchard a beehive

lost to fog

old woman
hurrying into darkness
dragging a shopping cart

listening to my
grandfather talking to his
radio

full moon –
and the sky a sea of
tranquility

ice along

the riverbank –   outlines

of winter

the blue wheelbarrow

1

blue wheel
barrow   filling with snow
beside the blackbirds

2

barrow left outside
by a man who doesn't garden
and never reads

new

moon   no

moon

snow fell last
night and now
Jacob's gone

birches

(in memory of Jacob Wigod)

yellow mist –
snow falling into
a blue river

fifteen syllables
converse with silence
on a white island

papers gathered –
empty room –
birches

Alexander Forbes

The poems of Alexander Forbes have appeared in journals throughout Canada from British Columbia to Quebec and across the U.S. from California to New York as well as in more than one anthology, including New Star Press's *Sentences and Paroles* and a selection of British Columbia writers chosen by Susan Musgrave. Co-author, with Tricia Sellmer, of *Rumours of Bees: Paintings of Tricia Sellmer, Poems of Alexander Forbes* (Red Heifer Press) he is also the author of *Oranges: A Novella for Puppets* (Gracesprings Collective). The biography of E.J. Pratt that he was asked to contribute to The University of Toronto *Encyclopedia of Literature in Canada* has recently joined his biographies of Alun Lewis and H.H. Munro (Saki) in *The Dictionary of Literary Biography* (Detroit). A prizewinner in the Artists Embassy International Poetry Competition (San Francisco), Forbes has been invited to give readings of his poems at the *Vancouver International Writers' Festival*, *The Shuswap Lake International Writers' Festival*, and many other festivals and venues in Canada and the U.S. Two CD's of his poems have been produced by Capitol Records gold-album recipient Henry Small (the former lead singer of PRISM), with readings by the celebrated singer and actor Tina Moore, known to many for her appearances in the Gemini Award winning *The Vetala: The Bill Miner Roadshow,* and *the beauty of the city in the last hour of the night.*